TRUE
Prosperity

Beloved, I wish above
all things that thou
mayest prosper and
be in health, even as
thy soul prospereth.
Beloved, I wish above
all things that thou
mayest prosper and
be in health, even as
thy soul prospereth.

JESUS IS LORD

KENNETH
COPELAND
PUBLICATIONS

True Prosperity

ISBN 1-57562-743-4   30-0550

10 09 08 07 06 05   8 7 6 5 4 3

Kenneth Copeland Publications
Fort Worth, TX 76192-0001

Beloved, I wish above all things that thou mayest prosper and be in health, even as thy soul prospereth.

3 John 2

TRUE Prosperity

In order to prosper, you must first have a prosperous soul. That's the beginning of the prosperous life. But how do you get there?

My journey to the prosperous life began years ago when I read Matthew 6:33 in a Bible Ken's mother had given him: "But seek ye first the kingdom of God, and his righteousness; and all these things shall be added unto you." In *The Amplified Bible* it says to seek "His way of doing and being right." That's the foundation of God's prosperity. When I found that verse, I was ready to try God's way since I needed a lot of things and my way wasn't working.

I discovered that God's prosperity isn't just financial blessings. It also includes healing, protection, favor, wisdom, success, well-being and every good thing you could possibly need—all the good things Jesus paid for you to have. He took our place and bore the curse of our sin so we can live in the blessing. "Christ hath redeemed us from the curse of the law, being made a curse for us: for it is written, Cursed is every one that hangeth on a tree: That the blessing of Abraham might come on the Gentiles through Jesus Christ..." (Galatians 3:13-14).

Isaiah 53:5 says, "The chastisement [needful to obtain] peace and well-being for us was upon Him, and with the stripes [that wounded] Him we are healed and made whole" (*The Amplified Bible*). The Hebrew word for peace in this scripture is *shalom*. It basically means "nothing missing, nothing broken," or wholeness in every area of your life—spirit, soul and body.

That kind of prosperous life doesn't just happen. And it doesn't happen overnight. But the foundation for true prosperity begins with these seven steps:

1. *Walking in truth*
2. *Faithfulness*
3. *Diligence*
4. *Tithing*
5. *Sowing*
6. *Believing*
7. *Saying*

So let's briefly take a look at each one of these key elements to walking in prosperity.

Walking in Truth

"I have no greater joy than to hear that my children walk in truth" (3 John 4).

If I told you about heaven, I couldn't give you any firsthand information because I haven't been there. But when I teach on prosperity, that is something I have experienced from minus zero to abundance. Kenneth and I have been walking by the laws of abundance for more than 30 years.

We weren't exactly walking in prosperity when we married. I wore a $2 veil with the white cotton dress my mother made for the wedding. Ken's friend married us at his home. His wife baked a cake. We even borrowed $100 for our honeymoon. We had no money and no wisdom. You would be hard pressed to find a couple that was more pitifully ignorant than we were at that time.

But then something happened that totally changed our lives. We began to hear the truth of the Word of God. First we got born again. We were changed inside, but outwardly you couldn't tell much difference in us. Once we were filled with the Holy Spirit, there was some outward change, but not a lot because we were still ignorant of the Word. The real changes in our outer lives came when we started walking on the

Word and letting the wisdom of God become our way of life. Everything began to change!

We found that the first step to increase is *walking in truth*. That means walking in the light of God's Word, according to His ways, His wisdom, what He says is right. You can't do that and not be blessed. Jesus said, "If ye continue in my word, then are ye my disciples indeed; and ye shall know the truth, and the truth shall make you free" (John 8:31-32).

I'm not just talking about reading scriptures about prosperity. You prosper when you walk in all the words God says to you. That's the wisdom of God.

Walking in truth is living a godly lifestyle—living in obedience to what God says is right. The blessings God outlined in Deuteronomy 28:1-14 manifest as a result of obedience. "And it shall come to pass, if thou shalt hearken diligently unto the voice of the Lord thy God, to observe and to do all his commandments which I command thee this day, that the

Lord thy God will set thee on high above all nations of the earth: and all these blessings shall come on thee, and over-take thee" (verses 1-2). God has always blessed an obedient people. Isaiah 1:19 says, "If ye be willing and obedient, ye shall eat the good of the land." God can do something with a person who has a willing heart. In fact Psalm 25:12-13 in *The Living Bible* promises that when you fear the Lord, "God will teach [you] how to choose the best. [You] shall live within God's circle of blessing...."

One of the first things God taught us was to stay out of debt—and we obeyed Him! That was big to us in those days. We started where we were and that meant believing God to pay the overdue bills. But increase came as we were willing and obedient to walk in the truth of the Word.

And increase can come to you also. God desires for you to live within His circle of blessing. It is His will for you to increase.

Faithfulness and Diligence

"His lord said unto him, Well done, thou good and faithful servant: thou hast been faithful over a few things, I will make thee ruler over many things: enter thou into the joy of thy lord" (Matthew 25:21).

The force of faithfulness is a fruit of the spirit that you received when you were born again.

Webster's dictionary defines *faithful* as "full of faith, believing, strong or firm in one's faith, firmly adhering to duty, a true fidelity, loyal, true to allegiance, constant in the performance of duties or services."

A faithful person consistently does what is right, even if it looks like it could be to his disadvantage. Psalm 106:3 says, "Blessed are they who maintain justice, who constantly do what is right"

(*New International Version*). We can't be godly without being faithful because faithfulness is God's character:

> It is because of the Lord's mercy and loving-kindness that we are not consumed, because His [tender] compassions fail not. They are new every morning; great and abundant is Your stability and faithfulness. God is faithful (reliable, trustworthy, and therefore ever true to His promise, and He can be depended on); by Him you were called into companionship and participation with His Son, Jesus Christ our Lord (Lamentations 3:22-23; 1 Corinthians 1:9, *The Amplified Bible*).

Second Chronicles 16:9 says God is looking for faithfulness, "For the eyes of the Lord run to and fro throughout the whole earth, to show himself strong in the behalf of them whose heart is perfect toward him...." The Hebrew word for *perfect* there means "loyal, devoted, dedicated, faithful."

Kenneth and I have had financial trouble, challenges with sickness and other things, but when we have stood on the Word and refused to give up, God has always answered our faith with His action!

Once you find a promise in the Word, don't disqualify yourself from receiving by saying, "God would never do that for me." Be transformed by the renewing of your mind (Romans 12:2). Let God's Word change your thinking. You will prosper in any area as your soul (mind, will and emotions) prospers in understanding about that area from the Word, and you take that knowledge and act on it. Your inner man prospers when you believe the Word. Your circumstances prosper when you receive what He says and act on it.

Be faithful to keep meditating the

promises in the Word until they overtake your life. Everything you receive from God starts with the Word in your heart. Proverbs 4:20-23 says, "My son, attend to my words; incline thine ear unto my sayings. Let them not depart from thine eyes; keep them in the midst of thine heart. For they are life unto those that find them, and health to all their flesh. Keep thy heart with all diligence; for out of it are the issues of life."

Faithfulness will energize you to be diligent even if you have never been that way in the natural.

The Word repeatedly says we are to *diligently* seek God, hearken to what He says and obey His commands. Why? Deuteronomy 28:1-2 says when you hearken diligently, blessings overtake you! Because "...he is a rewarder of them that diligently seek him" (Hebrews 11:6). Diligence increases you. As Proverbs 10:4 says, "...The hand of the diligent maketh rich."

Be diligent and faithful to God in

your natural life as well. Make a decision to be faithful on your job, at your church, in your prayer life and in putting the Word first place in your life.

Our soul prospers as we spend time in the Word, believe it and create a lifestyle of obeying God. The result will be what 1 John 3:22 says: "And we receive from Him whatever we ask, because we [watchfully] obey His orders [observe His suggestions and injunctions, follow His plan for us] and [habitually] practice what is pleasing to Him" (*The Amplified Bible*).

The number one law of receiving is *don't quit!* Stay with the Word. Stay with what God has told you to do.

Even if you make a mistake, repent and get back on track. That's faithfulness. It's part of the prosperous life because "a faithful man shall abound with blessings..." (Proverbs 28:20).

Tithing and Sowing

"Honor the Lord with your capital and sufficiency...and with the first fruits of all your income; so shall your storage places be filled with plenty, and your vats shall be overflowing with new wine" (Proverbs 3:9-10, *The Amplified Bible*).

Ken and I never had any financial growth until we became faithful in tithing. At first it looked impossible to give that 10 percent. But when we did, the 90 percent we had left went farther than the 100 percent we had before.

Tithing is a covenant transaction that gets God involved in what you are doing. The first 10 percent of your income—the tithe—belongs to God. The Bible calls it firstfruits. It's devoted to God, and it goes to support ministries that feed you spiritually.

Tithing is how you honor God with your money. It makes a way for God to bless you supernaturally.

Notice Malachi 3:8-10 says we are to bring *all* the tithes to God. It also says by doing so God will open the windows of heaven and bless you "that there shall not be room to receive it!" You don't want to keep anything that belongs to God. Leviticus 27:30 declares, "And all the tithe of the land, whether of the seed of the land, or of the fruit of the tree, is the Lord's: it is holy unto the Lord."

Real tithing is done with the heart and with the mouth, in faith. God's people were commanded to bring their first-fruits: "And thou shalt set it before the Lord thy God, and worship before the Lord thy God: and thou shalt rejoice in every good thing which the Lord thy God hath given unto thee, and unto thine house..." (Deuteronomy 26:10-11). They were to recount how God had delivered them out of bondage. And they were to worship Him and rejoice for all the good He had given them.

Whatever we do must be in obedience and in faith for God to be pleased with it.

Everything we do toward God must come from our heart. Otherwise it doesn't count. Jesus said, "It is the spirit that quickeneth; the flesh profiteth nothing," (John 6:63). We are to give with a willing heart, as an honor to God, and worship Him with our tithes. Then He is in partnership with us.

After we tithe, we are to sow according to what the Lord lays on our heart, and we are to do it with the right attitude. The Hebrew word for *offering* comes from a root word that means to "draw nigh." We draw nigh to God with our offering. Second Corinthians 9:6 says: "He which soweth sparingly shall reap also sparingly; and he which soweth bountifully shall reap also bountifully."

The Scripture plainly says you reap what you sow (Galatians 6:7). If you desire to be a receiver, you have to be a giver. "Give, and it shall be given unto you; good measure, pressed down, and shaken together, and running over, shall men give into your bosom. For with the same measure that ye mete withal it shall be measured to you again" (Luke 6:38). Tithing is supernatural—don't miss out on the benefits. God has an interest in your finances—He desires to increase you and bless you because He loves you.

Believing and Saying

"We having the same spirit of
faith, according as it is written,
I believed, and therefore have
I spoken; we also believe,
and therefore speak"
(2 Corinthians 4:13).

The Bible says several times, "The just shall live by faith" (Romans 1:17; Galatians 3:11; Hebrews 10:38). Abraham was blessed because he lived by faith. He believed God. We're supposed to live the same way: "So then they which be of faith are blessed with faithful Abraham" (Galatians 3:9).

Faith must be in two places—in your heart and in your mouth. "The word is nigh thee, even in thy mouth, and in thy heart: that is, the word of faith, which we preach" (Romans 10:8). Believing in your heart and saying with your mouth produces the operation of faith.

"For verily I say unto you, That whosoever shall say unto this mountain, Be thou removed, and be thou cast into the sea; and shall not doubt in his heart, but shall believe that those things which he saith shall come to pass; he shall have whatsoever he saith" (Mark 11:23).

Kenneth and I learned to take the Word literally as God speaking to us. We learned if we put it in our eyes, put it in our ears, and let it get down into our hearts in abundance, it would come out our mouths in faith-filled words and it would change our lives and circumstances.

We realized all that stood between us and walking in the dream God had for us was knowing what is in the Book and doing it. "This book of the law shall not depart out of thy mouth; but thou shalt meditate therein day and night, that thou mayest observe to do according to all that is written therein: for then thou shalt make thy way prosperous, and then thou shalt have good success" (Joshua 1:8).

The seven keys I've shared are how Ken and I laid a foundation for the prosperous life—and this is how we maintain it. I can tell you from experience, these are the first seven steps to increase, no matter what you need.

Prayer for Salvation and Baptism in the Holy Spirit

Heavenly Father, I come to You in the Name of Jesus. Your Word says, "Whosoever shall call on the name of the Lord shall be saved" (Acts 2:21). I am calling on You. I pray and ask Jesus to come into my heart and be Lord over my life according to Romans 10:9-10: "If thou shalt confess with thy mouth the Lord Jesus, and shalt believe in thine heart that God hath raised him from the dead, thou shalt be saved. For with the heart man believeth unto righteousness; and with the mouth confession is made unto salvation." I do that now. I confess that Jesus is Lord, and I believe in my heart that God raised Him from the dead.

I am now reborn! I am a Christian—a child of Almighty God! I am saved! You also said in Your Word, "If ye then, being evil, know how to give good gifts unto your children: HOW MUCH MORE shall your heavenly Father give the Holy Spirit to them that ask him?" (Luke 11:13). I'm also asking You to fill me with the Holy Spirit. Holy Spirit, rise up within me as I praise God. I fully expect to speak with other tongues as You give me the utterance (Acts 2:4). In Jesus' Name. Amen!

Begin to praise God for filling you with the Holy Spirit. Speak those words and syllables you receive—not in your own language, but the language given to you by the Holy Spirit. You have to use your own voice. God will not force you to speak. Don't be concerned with how it sounds. It is a heavenly language!

Continue with the blessing God has given you and pray in the spirit every day.

You are a born-again, Spirit-filled believer. You'll never be the same!

Find a good church that boldly preaches God's Word and obeys it. Become a part of a church family who will love and care for you as you love and care for them.

We need to be connected to each other. It increases our strength in God. It's God's plan for us.

Make it a habit to watch the *Believer's Voice of Victory* television broadcast and become a doer of the Word, who is blessed in his doing (James 1:22-25).

About the Author

Gloria Copeland is a noted author and minister of the gospel whose teaching ministry is known throughout the world. Believers worldwide know her through Believers' Conventions, Victory Campaigns, magazine articles, teaching audios and videos, and the daily and Sunday *Believer's Voice of Victory* television broadcast, which she hosts with her husband, Kenneth Copeland. She is known for "Healing School," which she began teaching and hosting in 1979 at KCM meetings. Gloria delivers the Word of God and the keys to victorious Christian living to millions of people every year.

Gloria has written many books, including *God's Will for You, Walk With God, God's Will Is Prosperity, Hidden Treasures* and *To Know Him.* She has also co-authored several books with her husband, including *Family Promises, Healing Promises* and the best-selling daily devotionals, *From Faith to Faith* and *Pursuit of His Presence.*

She holds an honorary doctorate from Oral Roberts University. In 1994, Gloria was voted Christian Woman of the Year, an honor conferred on women whose example demonstrates outstanding Christian leadership. Gloria is also the co-founder and vice president of Kenneth Copeland Ministries in Fort Worth, Texas.

Learn more about Kenneth Copeland Ministries by visiting our Web site at **www.kcm.org**

Materials to Help You
Receive Your Healing
by Gloria Copeland

Books

* And Jesus Healed Them All
  God's Prescription for Divine Health
* Harvest of Health
  Words That Heal (gift book with CD enclosed)

Audio Resources

God Is a Good God
God Wants You Well
Healing School
Be Made Whole—Live Long, Live Healthy

Video Resources

Healing School: God Wants You Well
Know Him as Healer
Be Made Whole—Live Long, Live Healthy

DVD Resources

Be Made Whole—Live Long, Live Healthy

Books Available From Kenneth Copeland Ministries

by Kenneth Copeland

* A Ceremony of Marriage
  A Matter of Choice
  Covenant of Blood
  Faith and Patience—The Power Twins
* Freedom From Fear
  Giving and Receiving
  Honor—Walking in Honesty, Truth and Integrity
  How to Conquer Strife
  How to Discipline Your Flesh
  How to Receive Communion
  In Love There Is No Fear
  Know Your Enemy
  Living at the End of Time—A Time
      of Supernatural Increase
  Love Never Fails
  Mercy—The Divine Rescue of the Human Race
* Now Are We in Christ Jesus
  One Nation Under God (gift book with CD enclosed)
* Our Covenant With God
  Partnership, Sharing the Vision—Sharing the Grace
* Prayer—Your Foundation for Success
* Prosperity: The Choice Is Yours
  Rumors of War
* Sensitivity of Heart
* Six Steps to Excellence in Ministry
* Sorrow Not! Winning Over Grief and Sorrow

*Available in Spanish

* The Decision Is Yours
* The Force of Faith
* The Force of Righteousness
  The Image of God in You
* The Laws of Prosperity
* The Mercy of God (available in Spanish only)
  The Outpouring of the Spirit—The Result of Prayer
* The Power of the Tongue
  The Power to Be Forever Free
* The Winning Attitude
  Turn Your Hurts Into Harvests
  Walking in the Realm of the Miraculous
* Welcome to the Family
* You Are Healed!
  Your Right-Standing With God

by Gloria Copeland

* And Jesus Healed Them All
  Are You Ready?
  Be a Vessel of Honor
  Blessed Beyond Measure
  Build Your Financial Foundation
  Fight On!
  Go With the Flow
  God's Prescription for Divine Health
  God's Success Formula
  God's Will for You
  God's Will for Your Healing
  God's Will Is Prosperity
* God's Will Is the Holy Spirit

* Harvest of Health
* Hearing From Heaven
  Hidden Treasures
  Living in Heaven's Blessings Now
  Looking for a Receiver
* Love—The Secret to Your Success
  No Deposit—No Return
  Pleasing the Father
  Pressing In—It's Worth It All
  Shine On!
  The Grace That Makes Us Holy
  The Power to Live a New Life
  The Protection of Angels
  There Is No High Like the Most High
  The Secret Place of God's Protection (gift book with CD enclosed)
  The Unbeatable Spirit of Faith
  This Same Jesus
  To Know Him
  Walk With God
  Well Worth the Wait
  Words That Heal (gift book with CD enclosed)
  Your Promise of Protection—The Power of the 91st Psalm

Books Co-Authored by Kenneth and Gloria Copeland

Family Promises
Healing Promises
Prosperity Promises
Protection Promises

* From Faith to Faith—A Daily Guide to Victory

*Available in Spanish

From Faith to Faith—A Perpetual Calendar

One Word From God Can Change Your Life

One Word From God Series:
• One Word From God Can Change Your Destiny
• One Word From God Can Change Your Family
• One Word From God Can Change Your Finances
• One Word From God Can Change Your Formula for Success
• One Word From God Can Change Your Health
• One Word From God Can Change Your Nation
• One Word From God Can Change Your Prayer Life
• One Word From God Can Change Your Relationships

Load Up—A Youth Devotional
Over the Edge—A Youth Devotional
Pursuit of His Presence—A Daily Devotional
Pursuit of His Presence—A Perpetual Calendar
Raising Children Without Fear

Other Books Published by KCP

Real People. Real Needs. Real Victories.
    A book of testimonies to encourage your faith
John G. Lake—His Life, His Sermons, His Boldness of Faith
The Holiest of All by Andrew Murray
The New Testament in Modern Speech by
    Richard Francis Weymouth
The Rabbi From Burbank by Rabbi Isidor Zwirn
    and Bob Owen
Unchained! by Mac Gober

Products Designed for Today's Children and Youth

And Jesus Healed Them All (confession book and CD gift package)
Baby Praise Board Book
Baby Praise Christmas Board Book
Noah's Ark Coloring Book
The Best of *Shout!* Adventure Comics
The *Shout!* Giant Flip Coloring Book
The *Shout!* Joke Book
The *Shout!* Super-Activity Book
Wichita Slim's Campfire Stories

*Commander Kellie and the Superkids*_{SM} Books:

The SWORD Adventure Book
*Commander Kellie and the Superkids*_{SM}
 Solve-It-Yourself Mysteries
*Commander Kellie and the Superkids*_{SM} Adventure Series:
Middle Grade Novels by Christopher P.N. Maselli:

#1 The Mysterious Presence
#2 The Quest for the Second Half
#3 Escape From Jungle Island
#4 In Pursuit of the Enemy
#5 Caged Rivalry
#6 Mystery of the Missing Junk
#7 Out of Breath
#8 The Year Mashela Stole Christmas
#9 False Identity
#10 The Runaway Mission
#11 The Knight-Time Rescue of Commander Kellie

World Offices
Kenneth Copeland Ministries

For more information about KCM and a free
catalog, please write the office nearest you:

Kenneth Copeland Ministries
Fort Worth, TX 76192-0001

Kenneth Copeland
Locked Bag 2600
Mansfield Delivery Centre
QUEENSLAND 4122
AUSTRALIA

Kenneth Copeland
Post Office Box 15
BATH
BA1 3XN
U.K.

Kenneth Copeland
Private Bag X 909
FONTAINEBLEAU
2032
REPUBLIC OF
SOUTH AFRICA

Kenneth Copeland
PO Box 3111 STN LCD 1
Langley BC V3A 4R3
CANADA

Kenneth Copeland Ministries
Post Office Box 84
L'VIV 79000
UKRAINE

We're Here for You!

Believer's Voice of Victory Television Broadcast

Join Kenneth and Gloria Copeland and the *Believer's Voice of Victory* broadcasts Monday through Friday and on Sunday each week, and learn how faith in God's Word can take your life from ordinary to extraordinary. This teaching from God's Word is designed to get you where you want to be—*on top!*

You can catch the *Believer's Voice of Victory* broadcast on your local, cable or satellite channels.

Check your local listings for times and stations in your area.

Believer's Voice of Victory Magazine

Enjoy inspired teaching and encouragement from Kenneth and Gloria Copeland and guest ministers each month in the *Believer's Voice of Victory* magazine. Also included are real-life testimonies of God's miraculous power and divine intervention in the lives of people just like you!

It's more than just a magazine—it's a ministry.

To receive a FREE subscription to *Believer's Voice of Victory*, write to:

Kenneth Copeland Ministries
Fort Worth, TX 76192-0001
Or call:
(800) 600-7395
(7 a.m.-5 p.m. CT)
Or visit our Web site at:
www.kcm.org

If you are writing from outside the U.S., please contact the KCM office nearest you. Addresses for all Kenneth Copeland Ministries offices are listed on the previous pages.